water

water

SECOND EDITION

COLLECTED POEMS BY
TIMOTHY F. CROWLEY

CHAPEL HILL
PRESS

CREDIT: The waterfall is a photo of a women-made back-deck project so treasured by the poet and his bride of many years.

Built with love during a three-weekend period, there was one who delegated with authority and an assistant who contributed by carrying stones far too heavy for the common person.

A very special gift to the future owner of the property, for everything changes. Doors open, doors close.

Copyright © 2007, 2017 Timothy F. Crowley
First Edition published 2007. Second Edition published 2017.

All rights reserved. No part of this book may be used, reproduced or transmitted in any form or by any means, electronic or mechanical, including photograph, recording, or any information storage or retrieval system, without the express written permission of the copyright holder, except where permitted by law.

ISBN 973-1-59715-140-5

Printed in the United States of America
Second Printing

Table of Contents

Eye Shadows ~ 1
A Chicken in Every Pot ~ 3
Paradise 1763 ~ 4
Discarded Beauty ~ 6
Mall People ~ 8
A Poem to an Old Lady Friend ~ 10
Immigration Tri-Fold ~ 12
Inmates Working ~ 13
Cousin Awa ~ 15
A Pierced Heart….1967 ~ 17
Winter's First Rose ~ 18
Sweetheart ~ 19
Aliento ~ 21
An Erotic Ode for the Elderly ~ 23
Spiritualis ~ 25
Spirit Sister ~ 27
Spirit Brother ~ 29
For M … (Form) ~ 30
Roundabout ~ 31
La Mesa ~ 32
Monday's Ashes ~ 33
Euclid Avenue ~ 34
Daddy Bluff ~ 35
Café Universe ~ 36
Family Matters ~ 37
Traveling Spirits ~ 38
Religious Convictions ~ 39
There Is… ~ 40

William Koster ~ *41*
Boxer's Body ~ *42*
Dolmen ~ *43*
Dusk ~ *45*
Worldview ~ *46*
Capturing Quixote ~ *47*
An Ode to all Poets ~ *49*
Changes ~ *50*
Bittersweet ~ *51*
Chivalry ~ *53*
The Covered Bridge ~ *55*
Sweet Voices ~ *56*
Secrets of the Heart ~ *58*
T.R.U.T.H. ~ *60*
Regal Runt ~ *61*
Mexican Spider ~ *62*
Pater Ave Atque Vale ~ *63*
One Potato, Two Potato ~ *64*
Ethical Conflicts ~ *65*
The Greyhound Guy ~ *66*
A Lost Poem ~ *67*
Wealth ~ *68*
Tillman—Texas 1978 ~ *69*
My Last Love ~ *71*
Weeping Roots/Silver Cups ~ *73*
Otherself ~ *75*
… "een-sehng" … "la vida" … "the life" ~ *76*
Relay ~ *78*
Whiteout ~ *82*
Cornerspot ~ *84*

Sometimes, I write in order to process my challenge with darkness and despair. At other moments, I write to celebrate joy. Also, I write to simply make sense of something. There are times when I write without knowing why.

Verse continues to guide me as I listen to the voices encouraging spirituality and objectivity.

This book, *Water*, is the final piece of a three-part collection. For this gift, I'm grateful and honored to once again pay tribute to my muse, my trophy wife, Martha Olaya, an incredible guide for our three children and their children, who has illustrated, through personal example, that anything is possible to achieve if one follows one's heart.

"Unhindered" by academic pressure, I'm seemingly able at any moment to cease working at verse.

Unfortunately, this is not so.

Voices come from everywhere.

A rhyme, a thought, a burst of energy all "force" me, encourage me to take writing instrument in hand to paper napkins, notebooks, shards of birch bark or cloth in order to cleanse the soul of its endless pit of poetic energy.

Both *Poets for Peace* and *Immigration, Emigration, Diversity* are complete and yet there's this compelling message to put into an immediate form a collection of verse I have chosen to call *Water*. Generational seeds have been planted. I cannot stop this flow. No one can stop the flow of water once it takes direction and determination. The title, *Water*, is symbolic for many reasons: while nations fight for oil and energy, and issues along with other self-serving resources, water—its contamination and incorrect availability and its necessary protection— must remind us it is our final source for survival.

There are messages within the lines. There's also a pattern of personal empowerment. Poetry, as we know it today, has endured many changes. It will continue to change and flow as it has since the beginning.

Poets and those who claim kinship have written many bits of verse: complete, somewhat complete, completely incomplete, and incompetently un-publishable, cast to storage boxes and ultimately discarded to the status of the fireplace or town disposal.

One day, while working on *Immigration, Emigration, Diversity*, an inspiration to begin collecting and stitching them into a fabric of sorts evolved.

And thus ... *Water: Collected Poems*.

TIMOTHY F. CROWLEY, *May 2007*
A primitive but professional working poet
Republished June 2016

water

Eye Shadows

Gentle eyes
resting in comfort's belly,
entrusting their shadows
talking with me.

Moving lips,
scolding playmates
they alone can see.
Smiling, bantering with
these imaginative beings,
chirping away, awaiting
Mother's return
puckering for an affectionate kiss
revealing secret relationships
behind the sofa, alone again.

Their little people category
protects them (unlike us)
in their innocence…

My lips cannot move.
I cannot chatter alone
amongst the elders.
I cannot reveal that which
my shadows have disclosed to me….

A Chicken in Every Pot...

ABIERTO
Beckons the traveler
to sustenance.
A menu of Southwestern flavor.
A place to soothe the palate;
so much more than ingredients.

A subconscious quest
for truth, hope, strength,
comfort, wisdom, compassion,
equanimity, sound health, and love.

Bring water to boil, simmer,
strain. Discard, slice, boil
again...
Combine, shred, boil one more time.
Simmer all of the above...

An ethnic penicillin...
Grandma's cure-all...
A bit of this, a bit of that.
All added to the commercial
boiling vat...

But for the soul
and with poetic license.
Possibly a smattering of
her magical powder.
A respite from the day…
One must find the way
to enjoy a taste
of Margaret's Chicken Chowder

Paradise 1763

Ripples on a silent water body
awaiting the evening hour.
Soon midnight's children
shall appear.
Weeping willows and their neighbors
Accept this silence.

A post home built by
human kindness awaits the pioneer.
Ice, bitter cold, winter's blanket
Are but a memory…

War, our most recent reference,
has also found a new home. It is here.
Now snipers, now terrorists, citizens all
full of immeasurable fear.
        Hopeless…
Armless
Legless
Eyeless

Set their sites on an occupying force.
We must pray for divine grace
Alas, the flow as we knew "it"
is no longer there.

Civilization and the children
of civilization must begin anew.
This is the summer place
Here is what once did not exist.
We must pray for divine grace
or we, too, shall disappear.

*(1763 is the address of George Washington's
summer house in Upperville, VA.)*

Discarded Beauty

Oh, she could dance.
An "adult" child
in an adult place…
A teen, contemptibly
surrounded by clever
subtle blue lights
and anguish drowned
everywhere.
Enter if you dare…

Oh, she could dance.
Water at $22.50 per glass.
"Dance?
Want a private dance Mister?
and for another $280, you could touch my ass?"
Do so if you dare.

Oh, she could dance…
The evening was warm
down South…
a sensual mouth
asking with carefully reviewed vocabulary
focused on unfulfilled affection.

If I chose to dance with her
I, too, would register my soul
as an adult child
in an "adult" place.
I double dog dare you…

Oh, she could dance.
I having the ultimate responsibility
for underwriting
one month's rent somewhere
for someone less fortunate
for ten "great" used books,
for knowledge is power, and
for one month's nutritional supply
caring for one dozen innocent babies
and to offer a glimmer of hope
somewhere...
I triple dog dare you.

Oh, she could dance.
It would have been quite shameful
of me to participate at
$22.50, a minor sum to pay.
I learned something new once again.
For shame—for $280 and
a moment of fantasy
which I chose to forego.
I double, triple dog dare you
to say no.

Mall People

Walmart, Kmart Shoppers,
let's attempt fairness here...
Kerr Drug dyed blue hair,
Ninety-nine-cent white sox climbing knees
covering winding varicose pathways
and bulging bellies, love handles (middle tires)
cursed by "Christy dream, Mighty Mac, and Hague
in the Dish Delish ice cream..."

Jogging with a cane
at a desperate pace,
window shopping in a place that is
quiet ... an early mall event
before opening time: at least an hour
when shopkeepers, overworked,
over "houred"
attend to the daily preparation
ashamed to join GI Joe's Gym.

A strikingly confident thirty-something Nubian beauty
passes by
magnificently attired
in her shop's clothing
which she was entitled to purchase
at 40 percent off, which is still too much.
It should all be free.
She's their gift.

Why try to fool her?
You can't.
Malls will be replaced someday.
Possibly neighborhood shops
will reappear
and the community we knew
will once again be dear.
Nothing is permanent…
Everything changes.

A Poem to an Old Lady Friend

An instant affair of the heart.
I, killing time, she behind
the window
waiting
flattened nose
to the plate glass.
Sweetly,
I suppose then
I don't remember the exact moment
she became part of us.

Yesterday
without asking for her paw,
He/She
began on their own.
She left her babies to our care.
We accepted
placing them lovingly.
This agreement was well in place
long before our eyes met.
behind the window with her
flattened nose
to the plate glass
Softly

Since that day
we have both lost a part or two.
She climbs bent branches now,
beckoning to me
for more attention
than safety…
She feigns deafness
unless needing to reveal a secret
or happens to be hungry…
Quietly
I emulate her.
Is she planning to outlast me?

Immigration Tri-Fold

∾ Fushia flowered One,
stoking, tearful, hissing,
earthly, farewell embers.
Embarking on a "coffin ship"
as morning light appears,
parents slip back into
twelve milkers...

Children's, children's, children's, children,
borne into a blissful, enlightened
social grace.

Ominous oceans carry heirs.
Human spirit spills into
overflowing water basins.
Life's source subsists
as oppression exists,
while the morning light of courage
of all humanity resists
and persists.

Inmates Working

Observing, understanding
freedom's illusion
by the side of the highway,
from the endless, scorching sun,
silent pines,
beyond barbed wire,
electrified fence, motion detectors
and technically perfect
back-up resources.

Our children, pieces of several
millions locked into
an industry overseen
by emaciated beaked-hat
bearing, mustached stereotype.
Degrees removed
from the guarded
with antiquated firearm
skull and bones
etched on forearm
Surreal.

Only accident of birth
enables us the opportunity
to avoid this Way
without Liberty.

Ready at a moment's notice
to discharge
at fast feet fleeing
or any attempt to disarm.
Dead on or destroying
another body part,
reacting to morning's
altercation with boss, spouse, lover,
another...

Our babies, without defense,
without sense - all spent
for free labor, under justice for all.
With message missent,
powerless against
Energy supported by
sub industries of black gold,
government sponsored drugs.
National defense —compassionless.

Cousin Awa

Awa bids good morning
Addressing me "percentage man."
I dig in for early
morning coffee change.

Alone by the extravagant indoor
waterfall created within the "belly"
of International Place,
adjacent to the World Bank…

A cast of thousands
traveling antlike…
Such subtle power…

How she knows who
I am, this Awa?
She smiles a sweetness—
a Third World Kind.

I know that smile.
I have encountered it
often on vacation.
That almost purple skin
belies all innocence and a
troubled mind.

I dare to consider Awa knows
all about me from CNN
and my insatiable greed
for instant gratification

of material goods, living
off her family's backs
"back home."

She … Awa, has found her way here,
Searching for a long sought liberty.
None other than Washington, DC.
I salute her and address her dark brown-
eyed genetic makeup of un-measurable
unbearable hurt
And courage…

Indeed I work for a percentage.
My most recent auto is parked for nineteen dollars
per day.
Awa sends that amount
home weekly
so her family and family's family
may survive…

Oh, she'll find her way.
"They" always do. Just
as our ancestors worked
their joy and their tears of sorrow
with the music of their birth.
I know Awa well!

A Pierced Heart... 1967

This young woman whom
I regard so strongly
lies on her stomach,
Outstretched, full length
On the sofa....
Her beauty, alone,
Leaves me helpless.
Darkened hair with
medium olive skin.
Such personal care
with lips of
the young nymph
destined to be
a goddess.

Beautiful, particular hands
calmly cover her chin and
the entire lower face, including
her lips are impenetrable.

It is her outstretched body,
which my eyes capture resting
the full length of the sofa,
which makes me afraid
knowing someday she
shall be claimed
by another.

Winter's First Rose

Is this an unplanned rose from
our backyard
sticking out her tongue
in anger, in tease, in trust
of a medicine man?
Is this post explosion of bloom
a petal awaiting its descent
to earth? Surrounded by
colors, converting from green to
red to spotted tan?
Is that a Man with a Gun?
How often within this season
do we have this scene within
our sight and not see it?
With a flicker, with a finger on a
trigger, we can start downward
all over again!
Let's see if this child can.
Let's see if this child can smile,
Let's see if this child can smile
once more.
Is it not possible to change
As the seasons?
Can we start once again
or is it just a rose?

Sweetheart

I hold you in my hands
in front of the mirror
of my mind.
"You're kind to me."

What do you wish
with this intensity?
To reproduce another you,
seeking eternity?
Hold me calmly in your hands
in front of the mirror
of your mind.

Am I hunted?
Are you the hunter?
Am I some fear-filled fantasy?
Can we coexist as one
extending kindness to our other being,
planning and planting
harmoniously?

Misusing all natural resources
requires we plan and plant as one.
With equanimity…
hold me in your hands
in front of the mirror
of our minds—peacefully.

Let us massage away
these layers of distrust, cynicism
and disrespect.
Allow these hands
and heart and mirror of the mind
to be one?

Hold me in your heart
in front of the mirror
of your mind.

Aliento

Brushed by Sidhe spirit,
wistful winds skirt silent streams.
Matador, gladiator, pugilist.
abandoned by entire entourage
countered deep
for Olympian courage.

Beast, braggart, jester
disloyal to the kingdom.
Nonresponsive to the palace
as war finds a fellow Enemy
displacing funds for
a never-ending other
War—Poverty.

Overused gods enter again and again
placing Race in the Face of mediocre men.
a breeze before a storm.
Roozenfeld, O'Crudelaich, Smith, Clay, Wayne,
Cursed for changing allegiance to a foreign god from
slave-given name.
The voice for an age; a messenger
whispering, poetically screaming defiance.
Jabbing at Death, crushing shame.

Bearer of Olympian myth
stripped clean.
Gory Glory, Peace, Everything,
Not bearing false witness to
those who
undermined him. We're one, two,
free. Co-existing Truth
and Spirit of Dignity...
Spirit of ancestry
Living the Personna

Breaking doors for Liberty
...
Ali....

An Erotic Ode for the Elderly

Let us sit cross-legged
naked
apart from the home.
Joining the magnolia, camellia, and wild vine
under the loblolly pine.
My hands holding yours,
Yours mine....

Actuarily, I'm weary
of the winks, blinks
twitches, witches, the nurses,
the preservation training
maintenance courses....

Marlboros, JW Black, or
Twinkies didn't do me in.
And nothing had anything to do
with SIN. It was
simply the genes.

We still have all our teeth!
May I caress your nipples
and toes and lobes
as
before the color blue
painted you?

May I suck as a child
with mother?
Is this wicked
under the pines??

I heard Security just
planted a camera
near the highway
the other day…
Old man Whoosie
crossed the street
Didn't look the other way…
Head on—the last one
In captivity…
The end.

Dedicated to all those who manage to avoid senior health care through murder, negligent family members, and profit mongering insurance companies.

Spiritualis

My love
Source
of all
that is…
Your pieces…
Parts of the cosmos
directing every move.
Body
housed in parts.
fingers, appendages
only shrink in contrast to your
most private places…
Swirling
within your sensuality,
feeling your healing
power throughout.
 A tongue reaches you
swirling also within you….
Nothing, nothing, nothing
manifests without paying complete
attention to your touch.
Your power brushes against me as
an autumn breeze
of warmth and chill.
Quiet, quiet moment follows.
not as quiet as the event itself…
Calm, calm follows the
softness of winter's blanket

as the lightness of waves
against the October shore
or against the left behind vessels
of an autumn gale..
Calm, following new mother's
giving birth, the baby
cooing in the mother's nest:
Calm, following a remote bombing of a bus
loaded with children, all innocent
victims removed to emergency wards
and burial plots
The spot is calm…
Oh lover … caress me now:
more than ever!

Spirit Sister

Layers of synthetic light
radiate evening's obscurity....
The womb of many waters
contains its secrets
from where we embark
transcending this mystery...

The world awaits
this courted being,
continuing its aggressive instincts
antithesis of peace
bearer of negligent chemistry...

Layers of humanity
depend and refer to
this impending glorious
calamity...

Spirit Sister
I reach out to you
searching for guidance, trust,
continuity...

Layers of water work their way
through mountain streams
boundlessness, washing away
suppressed whim, unfulfilled desire,
reproductive incompetence,
foolish fancy...

Courage … courage to risk the
climb beneath these generational layers
seeking an alternative energy:
a balance against the ragged edge,
fearful coexistence…

Layers of skin
defined by melanin
its purposeful demeaning
of ancestral reference
all in the guise of spirituality.

Violence, perpetual combat
sponsored by sport and greed
calling to the NAME in vain
sacrificing integrity…

Spirit Sister, my Spirit Sister
reach out to me!

Spirit Brother

Spirit Brother responds asking how Spirit Sister
trusts the voices of echoes, resonating
from the rooms of hell on earth

He believes Spirit Sister transcends
its existence

Spirit Sister teaches the words and the Way, encouraging
Spirit Brother to give oneself permission
To whomever will listen.

And if one receives this gift of knowledge and wisdom...
intellectual curiosity
VICTORY partners with the Spirit Sister.

FOR M ... (form)

Autumn leaves
Winter strives
Spring bursts
Summer thrives.

We must attend
to
EACH
Season
of
OUR
many
LIVES...

Roundabout

A recently acquired expression
for an ancient direction of a
simple circle.
And so we did…
Pointed by his energy
which in order to believe
you must concede to the concept
of chemical energy and quantum physics
Each moves seemingly without focus
guided by a common vision
of three who came after Him.
And the need to eat, to drink,
to seek mindfulness.
So to connect with a particular place.
Finding this place was not an accident
Roundabout—a recently acquired expression
of an ancient direction of a simple circle.

La Mesa

Weather-beaten, battered
ancient arbol.
Roots pulled by the winds
of autumn.
Set aflame for kindling,
rereading news of the
Northland
in autumn.
Living from memories, when a
rope hung from its strong limbs
and a child sang of autumn
in autumn.

Written during the year of Don Lechero

Monday's Ashes

Passed through the window
to the back seat.
The overcast and day's rain
dampened again
the bronze engraved box
in Mother's hands
so tenderly.
She held him again,
but not against her breast.

Together, they laid him to rest
in a carefully chosen spot.
A baby's lot. For it
was their baby's lot.
And the silent scar shall never leave.
The memory, the hope of youth,
the search for truth, the how, the why
will pass them by.
Mother and father move on—but your silent scar, baby
flashes,
your life blood for the moment,
is Monday's ashes.

May 31, 1982

Euclid Avenue

Out here in the Midwest
I'm in room number twenty-six—and it's private
Down the hall there's a queen
recovering far away from home, or dying.

Also on the floor there are
many rooms assigned to family
and guards for a King
from a Petrol Potentate.

I'm in good company?
The moment passed so fast—
it was hard to grasp—
as the King looked at me.

I was on the way to do what
he probably just did.
I know he caught my eye.

But he quickly turned straight ahead.
I didn't even try to acknowledge him.
He was just a King.

Cleveland Clinic 1978

Daddy Bluff

Daddy Bluff
negotiates asphalt pathways.
Hesitates at crossroads
with trees' black shadows.
At 4:00 AM
past luxury trailer parks,
once lush meadows

Daddy Bluff
lends chase as miniature humming birds
in search of red in the
garden of his mind.

Daddy Bluff
dreams of other times
and future ways.
He plants another tree.
He waves hello graciously
to neighbors passing by.

Returning nightly
Daddy Bluff ascends the driveway
knowing there's a better way
and true wealth is in the kin.

Daddy Bluff
doesn't allow
personal thoughts to enter in.
The choice was made
in the AM

Café Universe

Confabulations, ruminations,
toxic sensations,
disguised by Johnny Barleycorn;
and the eloquence of 100 proof
is proof enough.
The liver first and then the brain,
or is it the reverse
at Café Universe?
Momentary greatness drops to its knees.
One song, one ballad,
and one poetic thought, blessed
by one moment in the sun.
A pound of feathers, and
a pint is a pound the world around
is as a pound of stones (bar talk),
thud to the lines of verse.
Profound thoughts dissipate
into a new state
at Café Universe.

*Honoring the extinct patrons and those in hiding
of Barsanti's of Boston.*

Family Matters

I came upon a ragged soul
Homeless in attire,
Back against the wall.
He asked of me
Shamelessly for
some kindness.

Moving past him
more than a dozen steps,
there came a flash!
An instant recall. A referee, an open field
and swiftness of feet previously unseen.

I turned without my athlete's swagger
It left me long ago
Hand in pocket, new found kindness,
Shameless passion
and ready cash.

He was gone, our eyes had touched.
Our youthful memories as playmates
on life's fields passed into
this ever so fleeting moment of time.
Oh brother mine!
Oh brother mine!

Traveling Spirits

Hotel lobbies and
Airport terminals share
A unique bond.
The human spirit is everywhere.
Reaching beyond,
Seeking the known,
And the unknown.
Newspapers from out of town
carry incidents and clips,
of inclement weather,
sports heroes and city states
under siege.
Desk clerks and ticket agents
provide passage
for a moment's reprieve.
A brief nap, a two-hour flight
carries its passengers into the night.
Hotel lobbies and
Airport terminals share
the human spirit everywhere.

Awaiting a yearly review
sometime ago, from a hotel lobby,
observed Stan late for his appointment as usual.

Religious Convictions

Saints' tears flow
down cement columns,
covered with mahogany.
Whispers from boxes
lining walls cloak
the sins against each other,
defined by power brokers,
tied to God against
new cults in search
of the Lord.
Polytheism rises from the
ashes of asphalt. Plastic
photos found in Mother's attic
return me to a time
when youth and vigor defined
monotheism, with whispers from boxes
and crimes against the Lord.
Saints' tears flow
as rivers work their way
downtown under the asphalt and plastic
to the sea.
Saints' tears always flow to the sea.
Renaissance reaches out to me
with Saints' tears.

There Is....

There is ... I know—
this to be true—
the child in you.

Kindness and innocence
If only for a moment
I simply
know this was once us.

"Breathing in, I calm my body
Breathing out ... I smile.
Dwelling in the present moment"
I know this to be true
You can find the child in you.

Borrowed from the teachings of one of my heroes, Thich Nhat Hanh.

William Koster

Through my lens I depict—click
Tracing the path of a child's end—click, click
It's melancholic and true
The green grass is everywhere.
The music is happy. Little boy tries
to laugh, but can't in pain.
The magnified animals sing, dance,
and say, "Hello, what's your name?"
Unbearable pain. Music plays again.
A little one is quickly, quietly wheeled away.
It's not fair to the others
who all want to play.
I capture the moment, I depict—click, click.
The contract is over, but one more dance.
The kids return to their rooms
some, very few, have another chance.
The green grass is everywhere—click.

Eventually Dana Farber Institute was constructed. Created while consulting for the Jimmy Fund and Dr. Sidney Farber.

Boxer's Body

Left double jab, he danced
as he turned his back
to shouting fans (they
meant nothing to him).
So graceful. Tap, tap, tap.
He dipped to his right
and Bozo stepped forward,
catching thunder under the chin—
Yes, he was graceful,
and powerful. Bozo's
man placed his blade
into Boxer's body
as lights went dim.
His weapons of wealth
would never again witness
the count of ten.
Fans scattered.
Dreams shattered.
Boxer's body meant
nothing to them.

Dolmen

Barren walls.
Without floor covering.
A dirty, dusty clean—
The ballerina sweeps by.

Sitting, body crunched,
with arms wrapped around my knees.
I watch as she passes.

The floor is painted a path of
cleanliness. He follows.
They are Youth/Innocent youth.
The youth I knew.

I close my eyes and inspire.
Then expire again.
There are trees, from buds of green
to autumn, to pre-winter flight: A stream
of bordered snow, to a fast flow.
Uncontrolled to lazy, listless days of August.

September's warning with January halting
everything.
An overcast brings the boat to its mooring—
Caution—and the mountain path from spring
sponge

to summer powder, to winter hard,
reminds me, relaxes me—advises me
inspires me—

Autumn is near. Autumn is here.
Let me grow graciously
I need another season. I shall not go stale
I exhale—the tension
and fear that brought me here
is gone for now.

DUSK

delves into evening's shadows
PARENTS
await once dependent
BABIES
conceived within the confines of now lost
LUST
ECHOES
down pathways and crosswalks
LOVE NOW
for tomorrow is but a

WISHFUL
DREAM
which works its way downstream
TO MIST
LOVE
LOVE NOW
so you and you
ALONE
will never refer
again to all you
MISSED….

Worldview

That person looks just like me
Not exactly.
His eyes are brown, his hair kinky.
His lips are thick and his skin has
more melanin.
Not exactly.
The nurse is taking from him
what she took from me.
His blood runs red.
That person looks just like me
Exactly!

Following a serious auto accident when life left me for a moment written down from an ICU in California, 1962.

Capturing Quixote

Troubadours continue amidst
Squelched myths....
Mendacity seeped within
historic dust filled pages.

This the millennium
of rising tides,
unfolding, unmasking
unleashing. Unyielding
various truths, prevailing amongst quixotic
quests in search of bulgered,
sadamosamic positions
previously seeded by powers that be.

Flailing away at windmills...
Bringing chaos to the unsuspecting
innocent...
Paunched motley fools
knowing all along
it is falsehood.
Self-centered ignorance rules the roost
as avarice substitutes for sexual
non-fulfillment,
for sensual
touch, for
unrequited love.
Delusion replaces fantasy

and all comes to naught…
Barnyard after all.

Children acquire tiers of madness
and catch
this disease.
While the house of David and Benjamin
patiently awaits the beginning,
unlike a house of cards,
to complete the end
of the assassination
of the Sacred Feminine…

This is a harsh piece.
I dedicate it to Martha and her girls Anacristina and Natali
Jaki and her girls, Imani and Eva
Maureen and her daughter Quinn
Molly and her daughter Missy
and my spirit sisters, and all who believe in the power of the sacred feminine.

I suspect I'll recognize the sacred feminine when it touches me
Layers upon layers have peeled thanks to my spirit sisters.

An Ode to All Poets

Oh enemies of "mendacity"
(a word acquired from Poet Pablo)
who taught me "sacerdotal"
hopelessly living for verse.
and to my poet friends
Billy C and other descendents
of the old sod.
I digest their metaphors
their music as a sacred meal
through them and them alone
I praise God and her children
sifting through their bags of stuff
garbage … a seed surfaced
a glorious flower arises
in search of the sun
life begins
unloved "there's another one"
uncovering
fertilizing
germinating
evolving … truisms
there's another one!

Changes

Don't ask me to leave you.
I know their waste is poured
upon your heart.

You have changed markedly
during our time together.
I still recognize you—the central force,
and meaningful. This is the stable attraction
I retain and continue with you.

You—you're so brilliant, even
with those who use and abuse
your potential.
Your straight ashen hair is
now curly brown and black.

What once was, isn't—yet the greatness is there.
I still love you.
That which was so young,
now seems so much older.

Yes you and I have both changed.
But we understand and for this
dear Boston, I do still love you.

*1982 on planning to leave the property I promised
never to leave.*

Bittersweet

Market Aisles transport the traveler
as did the Silk Road...
Merchants and their wares
echo from distant chambers
these voices of lost years.

Ancient odors fill the air
joining hands when Earth was Mother
seeing when sight was keen
and sounds were seen when nothing was there.
Tastes, bittersweet everywhere.

Which path for the traveler is more secure?
The Silk Road
or this traveler's path
Which brings me here?

The Home of Abraham
divided as our own family members choose to be.
Modern medicine predicts what we were once
privy to know naturally...
Mind's power gently directs this prediction
to other places
no one person dares to go.

Oh dear Natural Being!
Native Americans
named you "Twisted Spirit"
with all your beauty…
In our vase once free.
Now contained…
You are ours to hold, to implore,
to caress, to teach, to see.

I reach out for the brass ring…
Once again … it is winter.
My horse gallops in silence up and down.
The park music plays sweetly.
I miss the brass ring and exit the marketplace.
A great wave covers all in its path
reminding us
how tentative is the human race.

January 2005

Chivalry

Another language of
an age long past, as
we enter
the new millennium, we ask
and answer.

It has not left us. We cuddle
great hopes, capture kind thoughts,
sustain intricate confidence
and retain fond memories.

To my daughter, and now
their daughter.
To their son, and now
our son.

With unmeasured gratitude
for the collective positive
teachings of those before us.

There's inspiration, generosity
and great hope for all of us
to comprehend,
as life's river winds the bend.
Chivalry … another language
and yet it's ours.

"I do" a sensitive, powerful
passionate choice.
I pledge all of mine to you

To Anacristina and Pat on their wedding day
September 1, 1996
Love, Dad

The Covered Bridge

The Covered Bridge
Protect me—
Cover me with your kisses.
This winter evening, love's mist of bussing noses
and touching lips
as the mail coach driver and his trusting steeds
seek safety.
While the windswept storm from the northeast blankets
its rooftop, hold me.
Wait out this force; Spring is soon to be.
Patiently, truthfully, lovingly.
The river rages beneath us. We're safe in one another's arms.
Mindfully, we watch babies nesting within its rafters.
Summer intuitively energizes and encourages us to
challenge the seasons next. It's autumn and winter again—
This is our covered bridge.

Dedicated to Natali and Chris on their wedding day.
August 19, 2000
Love, Dad

Sweet Voices

"May you sing and dance together but let each one of you be alone."
The Prophet on Marriage by Kahil Gibran

Let us listen for sweet voices
amidst the clamor of modern day.
A drummer plays to the rhythmic beat…
Our feet
Begin to find the rhythm
and a child's voice
is heard.
There's laughter,
there's celebration,
there's innocence,
there's gaiety.
Our life is once again revered.

The children each from their own garden.
tilling their way to parenthood.
Swiftly flowing as smooth as any mountain stream.
A child from one garden joins another
and life's joys and pains are shared as team.
Alas … Let us listen for sweet voices
amidst the clamor
of modern day…

Imagine the first meeting!
First eyes on one another
First words
First laughter
First touch
First sigh
First discomfort
First forgiveness
First goodbye…

Quinn and Galen…
We wish all of this for you.
Invite this sweetness
of the voices of your childhood when
you hear them talking … this is true
love…
Is all of us at this moment in your garden

To Quinn and Galen
on their Wedding Day
June 25, 2005

Secrets of the Heart

The perfect time always exists
to celebrate the moment of marriage
of two becoming one with bliss...

Siblings and loved ones
have left us scattered to the winds
as rowboats from their moorings
enduring a summer evening's
tumultuous storm...

Entrust your love for one another.
For it will direct your course
and bring you safely home...
Allow the spirit of loved ones
to sing with joy, laughter,
completeness...

Entrust your heart, for your heart
is the keeper of all secrets…
Elated, Olga and Carlos have
found one another...

And tomorrow, as today, each
will find the secret of the heart as lover.
Celebrate love openly as we know it
and may its spirit direct its course
even as the rowboat tugs at its mooring
during each season's storm…

For it is pure love that transcends
every living thing!
Every living thing!
And for this reason we
celebrate with you today...

To Olga and Carlos on their wedding day
Translated by/with "Everyone" in Bogota
March 16, 2002

T.R.U.T.H.

With a flashlight in hand
I roam the back streets
of the city
After three, it has been
called the hour of the wolf…
I return home to safety.

It's 10:00 AM and I stalk
the stacks of books
of the city library.
Receding into a corner
with one in hand
I return home to safety.

It's the twilight of my life
I search the rhythm of my body
I know it's near—
I return home to safety.

Regal Runt

Does this solitary shrimp
of a hummingbird
outside my window
tasting a nectar treat
holding firm against
the blood red flower
as a traffic copter
hovering the highway
on the newsbeat—

know the Latin translation
of the flaming midday meal,
as did Father?

I'm at the kitchen table
watching, sucking at
sweet iced caffeine laden tea,
protected from the silent
summer sun.

What can I learn
from this undersized
airborne runt of a
natural flying machine?

A magnificent sight
for a dog day
August afternoon
dream!

Mexican Spider

The Mexican spider sat down
beside her,
with other family members
and spun a web.
This Latin spider's goal of great
financial success
is somewhat overshadowed
by family and interdependence.
Nevertheless, this web,
spun together, as opposed
to its northern neighbors…
with indiscreet cannibal (spider
speak), eventually captures
prey and shares all of it
as a family.

Pater Ave Atque Vale
(Father, You Came and You Left)

Tearing eyes could
not keep me from
raising the un-watered
geranium stocks
placed at your plot.

And planting a black and white
photo under the once freshly planted pot.

A cinema scene
again provoked the tears.
I was not close enough
to check the photo from
years ago at your site.
I have removed myself from this
incredible sadness
which attacks
always in October.

One Potato, Two Potato

Phytophora
Infestans
Glocomora
Instant Americans
Crossed the bay
one by one.
I smell the blood of an Englishman.
From Erin to Botolph's town,
The mix began.
A Shea you're not,
You're a Kerry man.

Chibchas—and descendants
from the Pyrenees,
creating their own nuclear
pioneer families.

Fearlessly building new
frontiers…
Authentic pioneers,
awaiting another century
and millennium.

God save the Queen
for it was she,
who unaware,
brought you to me.

Ethical Conflicts

The gust slaps my face
It is the same force
that methodically moves the measure of time.

The Earth casually, comfortably, imminently
breathing spring's newness,
autumn's maturity and
winter's stillness.

I rub the grass against
my naked body. Its
oils and colors enrich
my liberty.

I reach for an apple.
The crunch noise startles
the peaceful moment.

A phone rings and a new mood appears.
Nature returns
to its origin. I move
further away.

The Greyhound Guy

⁓ Papers forged
he transported lonely,
wandering, isolated travelers.
En route,
listening for noises
of opening, rustling
brown bags,
resistant bottle caps,
leaking gasses,
wheezing breathing,
self whispers, hopeless sighs.
He became their guardian.
their sole source of
safety.

I knew him as the Greek in '57.
He became Demosthenes later in life and a college professor.

A Lost Poem

This piece escapes me
and works its way to the door.
I scramble to reach for its shoulder.
There's tugging and pulling.
I scream, "There's more!"

"Don't go out so fast," I say.
"Don't just go away!"

Wealth

Cosmopolitan, unlike those
resting near a river's bend.
The old man on the park bench
could no longer pretend.

Passing out bread bits
from his canvass bag;
tattered clothes defined
his ups, downs and current lag.

He rejected modern standards long ago.
Depression attacked him more
than in his head.
Friends
known in the better times
thought him dead.

Alone he found his long sought goal,
a road he always queried.
He never before did what he wanted,
too busy making money, worried.

The phone stopped ringing months
gone by. Postbox registered vacant.
Aged man's heart was lighter now—
at last he was a vagrant.

Tillman—Texas 1978

Mike Tillman plays a saxophone and a fife.
He played with Blood, Sweat, and Tears—and
walked away. He had to make it on his own.
It's early 1978, and much too soon to tell,
especially since success comes from within. This
minute inspiration causes me to express to
you this message from he who dares to be
opinionated, to challenge, to feel: Please don't
waste time. Understand and anticipate change to be special.

To: Olga Lucia, Manolo, Juan Carlos, Sergio,
Anacristina, Kali E., K.C., Jack, Natali, Karen,
AnaMaria, Maria Carolina, Peggy Ann,
Dennis Macho, Kahli P., Rasheed, Andres X.*

Who dares to challenge mediocrity
who moves with the sound of rhythm?
It must be you.
It must be him.

Please, our children, friends, grow with strength
and dare to attain:
Be a racist, a human racist
to gain full momentum.

Provide for all you have,
prepare for all you give.
It's love, and hope, and anxiety.
Provide, prepare your own new society.

Conquer, but love
and carry forth loyalty.
Gather within your nuclear family.

Go beyond—avoid complacence
With timing, fate, and patience.
You will pass on that which
I tell all of you:
The world is yours—
and to yourself
be true.

*Entered this world 3 years later!

My Last Love

Each day I visited her changing colorful dresses
and hair to match.
Superstore designer glasses
with a winking eye and
smile of innocence confused
my reticence and fear
as pounding heart and cautioning soul adored
her constantly changing
colorful dresses and hair
to match superstore designer
glasses.
Each day took strength to ask
as I visited her, the one
question needed to know,
to break the pattern of
thinking and reaching developed
as I passed a note to her
requesting not to open until
days end: And all
the spirit I felt and
strength I garnered
dissipated on Monday next
as I visited her, anticipating colorful dresses and
hair to match superstore
designer glasses. Heart pounding, the door
opened, the name

plate removed, a loose question
became a cannon within my
heart as I asked about her. She was
transferred with her husband. They're not
sure and the changing
dresses, designer superstore
glasses, and hair to match, became fact.

Weeping Roots / Silver Cups 2006

Am I preaching to the choir?
Or to those at least open to lend an ear,
Feel, simply feel and observe. Crows, large
black fugitives spot my auto crossing
the once virgin Potomac on a bridge
named for an early American hero of song
and verse, whose son was taken down by
a scoundrel, who had Lincoln's ear.

Did you hear what I observed
and felt years ago?
Am I preaching to the choir?

I have been told those must have been
the last of their kind
to leave the poverty
and shamelessness of those
they left behind.

My bumper sticker (everyone seems to have one)
Says: "COEXIST," but with whom?

Fugitives from injustice return from where they fled
centuries ago.
The Dismal Swamp?
The University Towns?
The State House?
The Multitude of Churches?

Tobacco shacks replaced by chicken and pig farms
local, political, and religious clowns?
Impersonators all
biding their time and wasting ours!

Am I preaching to the choir?

As crows follow my license plate down
Route 95 to 85 to my private place
and then to the Haw, the Eno, or up to the New,
the body of water heading upstream North.
escaping what began on the West Nile.

While the woman to whom I'm deeply endeared
returns from her journey to her homeland.
During this time I cut into ancient oak tree
roots, whose veins flowed,
now weeping. Roots planted
long before I came to be.
She brings back silver cups from our wedding day
she had innocently traded with her sibling.
I shall take one and go to the river close by.

Drink, drink one cup as the water flows, forewarning us
of our shortcomings and at the river's bend
My day once again comes to an end.

Otherself

Reappears without invite,
chattering away as though
in a vacuum, cast to the winds
and ravaging sea rudderless,
to and fro, side to side, sinking as any vessel,
waves crashing without
        respect for safety, rising for the ultimate
Gasp…again and again. Nights
turn to days,
Days turn to night
Wriggling muscles and nerves
Withstand and challenge this
ordinary timeless plight.
Asking me, ordering me to resolve
A courageous, endless, weakening,
        fight.

Dedicated to Nikki…August 2015

... "een-sehng" ... "la vida" ... "the life"

⤴ A meandering pathway
of eternal fragrance.
Gardenia, flower of North Carolina, accompanies
Andres source of beauty
And second home of the journey...
following
Fuschia of his elder, gracing the
Kingdom of Kerry.
Determined salmon
finding their way upstream
from the fearful Atlantic's
challenge.

Moments ago the sole
pathway to freedom also
the powerful Pacific
to another world of beings.
Sarah's Sacred flower
Calla lily adoring friend of
Hibiscus, follows...Oversees.
Sakura masu flow with their own grace,
Guarding mountain streams...confident.

Two distant lands join, once oceans apart.

Two cultures strayed eons ago.
When all earth was one.

Hands now touch from across both seas.
Earth-land minuscule compared to earth-water,
Join once again.

"La vida" … "life" … "een-sehng"

Dedicated to Sarah and Andres on their wedding day, Sept. 26, 2010

Relay

Joined arm in arm.
I believing our afternoon walk would eventually
be reached by auto.
To my surprise and delight she led the way.
With car keys in my pocket went with the flow.

She was in a calm place, content
positioned to walk a path travelled many times before by
dogs, wives, husbands, lovers…all seeking solace of some sort.
It was the perfect North Carolina January day.
Unusual warmth conquered the typical anticipation
of this month's history of chill.

As we entered arm and arm, she trying to respect
my pace, let go and
moved briskly to her own comfort zone.

We soon stopped to read a sign the pathway, historically
a Horse and Buggy Race track, evolving
into a NASCAR site.

Today, was not the day for the casual walker on this pathway
through the forest seeking calm. It was not a path for people to simply
walk, trot or run amongst the fertile land with wintery trees and
plants few could identify as could my Dad and horticultural
compatriots.

On this day it was a glorious opportunity
for my bride of 46 years as well as for me.

Recently modern medicine discovered a way to
 recreate breath as
a rebirth. New breath, long awaited and in a way still
 tentative with
fear, our enemy.
I loathe that word "fear" as breath is all each one of us
owns to enjoy or destroy with opioids, alcohol, tobacco
 or senseless
common, altered chemically enhanced food
products, even a wild animal on the path would avoid.

The gate in front of the path posted "closed until 4 p.m."
No walking available at this time on this path.
Soon observed a competition consisting of various
running clubs of many colors, genders, ages and
 audience members.

The curious or encouraging were with their team to win the relay.
It was unlike any relay race I had ever seen as
I was indeed a relay champion at youth.
Apparently this goal was simply to finish and enjoy
passing the baton with affection and confidence with more than
enough time to simply recognize
the champion in each
other as racing competitors.

Cohorts seeking better health through
joy, cleansed by nature's lungs providing
oxygen and clarity of mind.

Soon my bride and I left but not without recollecting the ultimate
competition and severity of the past
as a midget relay runner, high school champion
at the old Boston Garden
and avid admirer of those swift of speed.
The Olympics of 1976, which I attended assured me
of all expectations for those who dream.
Few experience this joy of passing the baton,
an Olympian training method,
trusting the next and the best and then the next
fellow runner, baton in hand, crossing the winner's ribbon
en route, always striving to stay out front.

May God bless those who understood what was
happening to each one of them that day, simply
sharing teamwork by entering a Relay Race.
May a higher power protect my bride and me,
      whom have lived so long,
we, left and arm, having passed
the baton to one another time and again.

A reminder that life as we know it demands a relay relationship
between couples and friends to simply
challenge the true race called Time.

Her dream at the moment was constructing another
new garden with waterfall and plants from many sources.

In order to race one cannot rest and allow time to contradict the
need for blood flow and breath, for better or worse.
Springtime is moments away.
Breath is the ultimate gift.
Authentic devoted love to one's
spouse is a miracle in the making.
It is the garden, which continues
to offer optimism to those
who believe it is possible.

*To Martha, my beloved Racing Team Member
who has carried the baton with grace and honor for her
children and children's children.*

Whiteout

From a place above, a voice,
unusually tranquil, descends
"messengerless"…
Words of admonishment, advice
and well designed language,
without rage of race.
The color white is justly so,
a classification of color.

A color blending with others, creating,
fulfilling an unexpected sensation
of the wheel which blends into a more severe
darkness or sensual, luxuriously bright lightness,
providing curiosity and complete joy for the viewer.

Innocence for one is a definition, prominently
defined with whiteness.
Dark suggests without light yet light touches
each one of us with an image taught to us with
many possible meanings, none exact or truthful.

A young bride gently striding down the aisle to swear
forevermore, adorned in pure white with scattered rose petals
preceding her trail while family children still white, sweet and
innocent lead the way.

The color white alone suggests many shades.
Family members and friends gleaming
with joy, another colorful word.

Many connotations possibly interpreted
and individually processed by guests of
both the bride and groom.
A declaration of forevermore is jointly professed.
All cheer the new couple and the joyous moments
of dance and toasts to one another and blessed servings
of the wedding meal.

The cake! "Oh the cake!"
Sometimes cut before and sometimes after the main meal.
It's symbolism for sharing with one another for eternity.

This day, if blessed with adoration and love, whitened
with a commitment of two becoming
one forevermore, striving on into a promising, realistic
and joyful state of God's Grace.

Time continuing into hours, years, decades,
children soon arrive and another chapter begins.
This is an adventurous "fairy" tale shared by many
with some who simply cannot endure the trials
That encounter the fact it is not for everyone.
Blessed are those who believe
This dream surrounded by a multitude of colors stitched
with threads of white.

March 17, 2016

Cornerspot

It is two hours away from
Sunrise…in the real south.

Several challenges await the
person on the crosswalk, including
blinking traffic lights
which understandably can be non-
informative at such an early hour.

If a promising day, one might never realize
choosing to carelessly cross to the other
side with lunch pail, attaché, folio under arm.

There are many events in this thriving city
which welcomes all to appreciate.
Even the elderly travel with calm.
Youth is everywhere and pleasure abounds.

As commerce rules this place stolen by one of my tribal
members long ago, before the river became part of
a soothing sound of paradise.

Looking both ways, making choices at this Cornerspot.
Positivity proudly pointed to the place chosen
to spend several days aware challenges are everywhere:

to make something from nothing, but authentic
is the dream most beholden for
those who dare to dream…

For my bride of many years. Love,
Teemi